THE 3D GOSPEL
MINISTRY IN GUILT, SHAME, AND FEAR CULTURES

JAYSON GEORGES

What people are saying about
The 3D Gospel

"An excellent resource for all who work to frame the Christian message in any culture."
–Themelios (The Gospel Coalition)

"*The 3D Gospel* is a beneficial and recommended primer."
—Missiology: An International Review

"This book can serve as a starting place to explore the dynamics of these very real issues which, if taken seriously, will indeed enhance gospel witness to those embedded in a different worldview."
—Evangelical Missions Quarterly

"Jayson Georges, an experienced missiologist, shows how the good news of Jesus applies to a wide variety of cultures in *The 3D Gospel*."
—Southeastern Theological Review

"*The 3D Gospel* makes significant cultural concepts approachable and easy to see. Thank you Jayson, for helping people grasp the complexity of global cultures and its implications for Christian mission."
—Judith Lingenfelter (Ph.D.)
Professor of Intercultural Studies, Biola University

"Tired of evangelism models that produce legalism, nominalism, and/or syncretism? Jayson Georges' *The 3D Gospel* can provide some solid solutions."
—Tom Steffen (Ph.D.)

Professor Emeritus, Biola University

"I am excited that *The 3D Gospel* is now available. It is a practical guide for Christians who want to see how different types of cultures and worldviews influence how we read the Bible and develop mission strategies."
—Jackson Wu (Ph.D.)
Seminary teacher in Asia, author of *Saving God's Face*

"Jayson Georges' book is a must read for all Christians who love people from different cultures. *The 3D Gospel* is a concise presentation of the main cultural frameworks, for which the author proposes a coherent presentation of redemption. This makes it a very informative and useful tool."
—Florent Varak
Pastor in Lyon, France, professor at Geneva Bible Institute

"Jayson's insights are birthed from many years of experience as a practitioner combined with lots of biblical and anthropological studies. *The 3D Gospel* will be helpful for the lay person reaching out to their international neighbor as well as the veteran missionary that has been serving overseas....and anyone in between."
—Grant Haynes
Director of Global Frontier Missions

"*The 3D Gospel* is an excellent, eye-opening treatment of the guilt-innocence, shame-honor, and fear-power cultures. Jayson Georges' research, Scriptural insights, and use of these three worldview lenses is of great value to those of us who minister to and with the nations."
—Jeffrey A. Gill (D.Min., Ph.D.)
V.P. and Dean, Grace Theological Seminary

"With many of our worlds colliding — modern, postmodern, Western, Eastern, immigrant, expatriate, etc., *The 3D Gospel* provides the needed "color-correction" to our lenses when presenting the gospel. If you're wondering what might be missing as you communicate the gospel outside of your home context, read *The 3D Gospel* — there simply is no other resource like it. ... This is essential reading for the next generation of church and mission."

—David Park
Pastor, founder of Next Gener.Asian Church

"As someone who has worked with people from Central and East Asia, I find Jayson George's insights very helpful. Clearly written and practical, this book helps people take off their cultural blinders, understand others, and serve more effectively."

—Kitty Purgason (Ph.D.),
Professor in Cook School of ICS, Biola University

"For centuries the gospel has unfortunately been truncated to Western theology's one dimensional approach for all cultures and contexts. *The 3D Gospel* brings to our awareness the cultures of Scripture and our world. This is a necessary and foundational resource for helping us to realize and avoid cultural blinders that hamper effective cross-cultural ministry."

—Rev. Martin Munyao (Ph.D. student)
Pastor and theology teacher in Kenya

The Culture Test

For your learning benefit, first visit **www.TheCultureTest.com** and complete the 25-question quiz to learn your group's primary culture type. The free test takes 5 minutes to complete, and results are received immediately.

THE 3D GOSPEL
Ministry in Guilt, Shame, and Fear Cultures

©2017 by Jayson Georges

Published by Timē Press, 2017.

Originally published in 2014. Updated and revised in 2017.

ISBN-13: 978-0692338018
ISBN-10: 0692338012

At the time of publication, all articles, blog posts, and videos link cited in this book were available online for free. A citation does not imply an endorsement of all material, but simply relevance for further learning.

A 50% discount is available on all bulk purchases—50 copies for $225 USD. This book is also available in multiple translations. For information, visit at www.HonorShame.com/3DGospel.

Table of Contents

1
SEEING NEW REALITIES

Gulzel trusted in Jesus as a university student. The message through which she accepted Christ was fairly standard: "Your transgressions separate you from God; therefore you deserve punishment. Jesus died for your sin. Believe in him, and your sins will be forgiven." Her faith was genuine and real. Her sins were forgiven and she enjoyed new life in Christ. But as a Central Asian, Gulzel faced unique situations that forgiveness could not fully address.

One Sunday evening, Gulzel was returning to the city from her mom's house in the village. The taxi she entered had a male driver and three male passengers. After a short while the men began inviting Gulzel to their homes for tea and propositioning her. As a young girl she felt uncomfortable and tried to downplay the situation. Halfway through the ride, the men stopped for a round of vodka shots along the road. Being intoxicated, the men became physically aggressive. At just that moment, Gulzel noticed her uncle in an oncoming car, heading in her direction. But instead of jumping into the road and flagging her uncle down, Gulzel hid. She did not want her uncle to see her. Gulzel's primary concern in that moment was avoiding shame and maintaining family honor.

A few years later, Gulzel's brother died. Her family mourned the tragedy, especially since he played a unique role as the family's oldest son. A few weeks after his death, Gulzel began having regular dreams of her brother. While she was asleep, spirits in the likeness of her brother tormented her. When Gulzel mentioned the dark dreams to her family, she was told to eat dirt from the brother's gravesite to appease the spirits. Gulzel desired power over the spiritual realm to escape torment and find peace.

Though truly forgiven of her sins, Gulzel needed to experience God's salvation from shame and fear, as well as guilt. Gulzel, as with most Christians in the majority world, requires a three-dimensional gospel of God's forgiveness, honor, and power.

Three Types of Culture

Christian missiologists identify three responses to sin in human cultures. Eugene Nida said, "We have to reckon with 3 different types of reactions to transgressions of religiously sanctioned codes: fear, shame, and guilt."[1] These three moral emotions have become the foundation for three types of culture: (1) *guilt-innocence cultures* are individualistic societies (mostly

Western), where people who break the laws are guilty and seek justice or forgiveness to rectify a wrong, (2) *shame-honor cultures* describes collectivistic cultures (common in the East), where people are shamed for fulfilling group expectations seek to restore their honor before the community, and (3) *fear-power cultures* refers to animistic contexts (typically tribal), where people afraid of evil and harm pursue power over the spirit world through magical rituals.

These three types of culture are like group personalities defining how people view the world. Just as individual people have a *person*-ality, cultural groups share a *group*-ality. Groupality refers an "organized pattern of behavioral characteristics of a group."[2] A person's cultural orientation, or groupality, shapes their worldview, ethics, identity, and notion of salvation, even more than their individual personality does. For this reason, awareness of culture types helps us anticipate cultural clashes and communicate the gospel three-dimensionally to the world. The book of Ephesians is a good example of how God's grace remedies guilt, shame, and fear.

The 3D Gospel in Ephesians

Paul wrote the book of Ephesians to explain "the unsearchable riches of Christ" (3:8), which involves each of these three components of salvation (italics added below).

Guilt-Innocence—"In him we have redemption through his blood, the *forgiveness of sins*" (1:7a). God "made us alive with Christ even when we were dead in *transgressions*" (2:5).

Shame-Honor—"In love he predestined us to be *adopted* as his *sons* through Jesus Christ" (1:5). "You are no longer *foreigners* and *aliens*, but *fellow citizens* with God's people and *members* of God's *household*" (2:19, cf. 2:12-13).

Fear-Power—"That *power* is like the working of his *mighty strength*, which he *exerted* in Christ when he *raised* him from the dead and seated him at this right hand in the heavenly realms, *far above all rule* and *authority, power* and *dominion*" (1:19-21). "Be *strong* in the Lord and in his *mighty power*. Put on the *full armor* of God so that you can *take your stand* against the *devil's schemes*" (6:10-11). ← how interesting!

Three aspects of salvation also emerge from Paul's central prayer: "I pray that the eyes of your heart may be enlightened in order that you may know the *hope* to which he has called you, the riches of his *glorious inheritance* in the saints, and his incomparably great *power* for us who believe" (1:18-19). The gospel always remains an indivisible whole, but examining the facets individually provides a more complete understanding of salvation. Reading Ephesians three-dimensionally helps Christians fully perceive "the riches of God's grace that he lavished on us with all wisdom and understanding" (1:7-8). [3]

Seeing the Complete Diamond

The gospel is a many-sided diamond, and God wants people in all cultures to experience his complete salvation. But despite the multifaceted nature of Christian salvation, Western Christianity emphasizes one aspect of salvation (i.e., forgiveness of sins), thus neglecting other facets of the gospel of Jesus Christ. Imagine a diamond with only one side! For cross-cultural workers, *or even cross generational workers* a truncated gospel hinders spirituality, theology, relationships, and ministry. We unintentionally put God in a box, only allowing him to save in one arena.

Understandably, Western Christianity emphasizes the facet of biblical salvation most meaningful in its cultural context. Historically, two significant voices behind Western theology, Augustine of Hippo (b. 354) and Martin Luther (b. 1483), were both plagued with an internal sense of God's wrath toward their transgressions. So their writings explore how God forgives and acquits guilty sinners. While theology from Western contexts addresses guilt and innocence, people in most Majority World cultures desire honor to cover shame and power to mitigate fear.

Despite the prominence of shame-honor and fear-power dynamics in global cultures, they remain conspicuous blind spots in most Christian theology. Gulzel's understanding of Christian salvation, adopted from Western Christianity, was only one-dimensional. Consequently, she defaulted to cultural practices to access honor and power, bypassing God's grace. What is the gospel for guilt, shame, and fear contexts? What does the entire diamond look like?

The cultures of the biblical world were primarily shame-based and fear-based. Consequently, honor and power are prominent features of the biblical story. The salvation story of the Bible presents a theology and missiology for all three types of cultures. The contemporary Church must likewise present the 3D gospel in various cultural contexts. To equip global Christians for increased fruitfulness in ministry, we examine each group orientation culturally, theologically, and missiologically.

2
CULTURE

Maintaining Balance

Although guilt, shame, and fear are three distinct cultural outlooks, no culture can be completely characterized by only one. These three dynamics interplay and overlap in all societies. Gulzel's circumstances illustrate how Central Asian culture integrates shame and fear dynamics. Even individuals or groups within a culture can vary, depending on region, age, gender, etc. A rural Thai might be more fear-based than an urbanite in Bangkok. Young adults in America valuing authenticity and connection are becoming more shame-based. Human complexities defy simple, either-or categories.

A more accurate model of culture measures the influence of each dynamic upon a group. Observe the triangle below, with each corner representing guilt, shame, or fear. A group's cultural orientation, reflected by the position in the triangle, depends on how strongly each dynamic pulls upon the group.

Examples only for illustration, not based on actual research

Each cultural worldview is a unique blend of guilt, shame, and fear. So a shame-based culture is positioned *towards* (not *in*) the top corner. Roland Muller says the three dynamics are like the three basic colors from which artists create thousands of colors. How much of each color is used determines the final type of culture that emerges.[4]

Like all cultural paradigms, the guilt-shame-fear trichotomy simplifies complexities into categories for the sake of clarity. Though every culture is unique, they all possess some general traits that can be categorized into three culture types. The following sections summarize the common features of each culture type.

Guilt-Innocence Cultures

"Integrity is doing the right thing, even when nobody is looking."

—C.S Lewis

The notions of right and wrong are foundational pillars in guilt-innocence cultures. Society creates rules and laws to identify what actions are right and wrong. These rules and laws define acceptable behavior. A mature person knows right and wrong—she is a "law-abiding citizen." Doing right keeps one innocent; doing wrong makes one guilty. Governments, corporations, schools, and even families establish rules to guide social behavior and expect those rules to apply to all people. Nobody is above the law. Society expects blindfolded Lady Justice to always judge impartially.

Guilt-oriented cultures do not simply emphasize rules and laws but socialize people to internalize the codes of conduct. Moral responsibility comes from within. Society expects our internal consciences to guide us so we do what is "right." One of my earliest childhood memories was a tormented conscience for stealing a Hot Wheels fire truck from pre-school. Even though no one witnessed me, my young conscience tormented me until I returned it the next day. Guilt needs no audience.

The result is an individualistic system. Western parenting trains children to "think for yourself," "be true to yourself," and "blaze your own trail." Bowing to social pressure and blending in are rarely admired. People are autonomous. Since everyone possesses their own internal compass, individuals define acceptable behavior. Society expects people to act rightly by themselves.

But when a person does something wrong (as defined by rules and laws), justice requires those negative actions to be addressed in an equitable manner. Various phrases in English reflect the supremacy of justice in structuring Western society; when wrong is committed, we "seek justice," "demand justice," and require that "justice be served." Justice is a sense of universal moral rightness.

Guilt cultures focus on actions. A guilty violator can remedy a bad action with another action—community service, paying a fine, jail time. Since the problem is a wrong action, the solution is a counterbalancing action that fits the misdeed. To alleviate guilt, a person must typically confess wrongdoing and/or provide restitution. The person who honestly takes ownership of wrongdoing is rewarded. For example, a politician accused of marital unfaithfulness can typically repair the situation by publicly confessing wrongdoing. These interrelated concepts of introspective conscience, confession, right/wrong, restitution, justice, and forgiveness guide social behavior in guilt-innocence cultures.

The guilt-innocent orientation frames not only a culture's morality, but also influences concepts of human identity. Because of the emphasis upon actions, individualists derive value from "doing." Identity is based upon jobs and hobbies, instead of family or ethnicity. People define themselves by how their behavior and self-expression differs from the group, not by what group they are a part of.

[what I Do, is WHO I AM.]

The road to an individualistic, guilt-innocence culture in the West began more than 2,500 years ago. The ancient Greeks and Romans lived for honor; the virtue *philotime* ("love of honor") was highly regarded. But over time, the philosophers suggested that honor be ascribed for moral conduct, instead of lineage, athleticism, or wealth. Doing right, not just being powerful, should make a person respectable. In *Euthyphro's Dilemma,* Socrates concluded that even the gods should act piously. Ancient philosophers attached status to individual moral behavior.

Then later, Renaissance and Enlightenment thinkers defined people as autonomous, rational individuals: "I think, therefore I am." Western philosophy now explains a person's essence apart from their relationships or community. Consequently, Western civilization dismisses communal dynamics (i.e., honor, shame, and face) in favor of guilt, innocence, and justice.

Shame-Honor Cultures

"Honor is the good opinion of good people."

—Seneca, famous Roman philosopher

In the wake of the tragic Boston Marathon bombing in 2013, the media found the suspects' uncle. On public television, the Chechen uncle denounced his nephews; "You put a shame on our entire family—the Tsarnaev family. And you put a shame on the entire Chechen ethnicity. . . . Everyone now puts that shame on the entire ethnicity." As Americans roiled from the tragedy of loss, the Chechen uncle bemoaned his people's shame.[5]   *wow!*

Shame-honor societies assume a strong group orientation. Honor is a person's social worth, one's value in the eyes of the community. Honor is when other people think well of you, resulting in harmonious social bonds in the community. Honor comes from relationships.

Shame, on the other hand, is a negative public rating: the community thinks lowly of you. You are disconnected from the group. For example, one Thai word for shaming means "to rip someone's face off," such that they appear ugly before others. Here are the words of an Israelite lamenting to God about shame "You have made us the *reproach* to our neighbors, the *scorn* and *derision* of those around us. You have made us a *byword* among the nations, a *laughingstock* among the peoples. My *disgrace* is before me all day long, and my face is covered with *shame*" (Psa. 44:13 15, emphasis added)

Honor and shame function like a social credit rating measuring one's reputation. Because honor and shame are inherently relational, such cultures are collectivistic. Members of shame-honor cultures are expected to maintain the social status of the group, often at the expense of personal desires. If a young person marries into the wrong clan, the village eyes compel the father to act in the interests of the family's honor. Shame and honor are contagious; what one person does will affect the entire group. When Brazil lost 7-1 to Germany in the 2014 World Cup, Brazilian fans responded, "Our nation is hurt. We will need to face people making fun of us the rest of our lives," and "I feel ashamed to be Brazilian."[6] In the Bible as well, God's people shamed God's name (cf. Mal 1:6; Rom 2:24). At a young age, children learn they are expected to act as representatives who uphold the group honor. So, a person's aim is to avoid bringing shame upon his or her family, village, and even nation.

The social matrix of honor-shame cultures is designed around establishing and expanding a network of relationships. Connections are vital in every aspect of life. Who you know (and who knows you) is everything! Group-oriented cultures value relational harmony. People strive to maintain interpersonal bonds and avoid offending others. Saving face and keeping peace preserve connections.

In relationships, it is critical to maintain a balance in obligations and reciprocate. Gifts and hospitality are always repaid, lest one incur a "social debt" of shame before peers. Family dynamics and leadership structures are more authoritarian. People grant leaders authority and prestige in return for provision and protection.

In a shame-honor culture, every person has a proper role, which is often based on age, gender, and position. People maintain honor by behaving according to that role. Even children learn how to honorably navigate relationships or circumstances. Wesley Yang says the Asian "parenting style explicitly intends the humbling of the individual self in favor of the needs of the broader collective. . . . This parenting style aims at the creation of an 'interdependent self,' defined not by its sense of inner autonomy, but by its sensitivity to the social roles it must play depending on the context in which it finds itself."[7]

The group enforces morality externally. When making choices, people ask, "What is honorable?", "What will others think?", or "What about my family name?" When a person has multiple social roles, acceptable behavior depends upon the context, not the rules. Shame-honor cultures do believe in moral right and wrong, but define morality relationally, not legally or abstractly. What is best for relationships *is* morally right. (wow!)

While actions can produce shame (i.e., tax evasion, or tripping on stage), the deepest shame often comes from being a certain type of person. Status in collectivistic societies is primarily inherited from the group. Who you are, either

22

honorable or shameful, is ascribed based on your group's ethnicity, prominence, origin, and lineage. Identity is based more upon who you are than what you do. People from Asian cultures introduce themselves by giving their family name first. In the Gospels, Jesus bestowed dignity and honor on many who lived in shame due to circumstances beyond their control. The blind, deaf, lame, lepers, bleeding women, demon-possessed, and Gentiles were unclean outcasts whom Jesus restored physically and socially.

✻ the good news ✻

Shame produces feelings of humiliation, disapproval, and abandonment. Shame means inadequacy of the entire person. While guilt says, "I *made* a mistake"; shame says, "I *am* a mistake." Since the problem is the actual person, the shamed individual is banished from the group. To avoid such rejection and isolation, people mask their shame from others. The following chart compares how guilt-based and shame-based cultures shape behavior.

	Guilt-Based	Shame-Based
Normal defined by	Rules and laws	Relationships & roles
Behavior guided by	Internal conscience	External community
Violations produce	Guilt	Shame
Core problem	"I *made* a mistake" (action)	"I *am* a mistake" (being)
Violations Affect	The transgressor	The group
Violator's Response	Justify or apologize	Hide or cover
Public's Response	Punish to serve justice	Exclude to remove shame
Way for Resolution	Forgiveness	Restoration

Managing shame is essential because a shamed person (unlike a guilty person) can do very little to repair the social damage. Removing shame requires more than forgiveness. Correcting shame requires a sort of remaking or transformation of the self; one's identity must change. More often than not, a person of a higher status must publicly restore honor to the shamed, like the father graciously did for the prodigal son in Luke 15.

Westerners often miss honor and shame dynamics in other cultures. One reason is that languages use different words to talk about honor and shame, such as: glory, reputation, status, dignity, or worth. Many cultures use the metaphors "name" or "face" to talk about shame and honor, since people are known by their name and face.

Also, cultural expressions of honor and shame can appear contradictory. For example, Middle Eastern cultures aggressively compete for honor. Conflict is viewed as win-lose or lose-win. So they may resort to honor killings or even terrorism to avoid shame and restore honor. But far Eastern cultures, such as Japan and Korea, strive for harmony. Conflict is a win-win or lose-lose game. So East Asians respond to shame by withdrawing or even committing suicide. Though the outward expressions contrast, both cultural blocs are deeply rooted in shame-honor values. [8]

Fear-Power Cultures

In fear-based cultures, it is not important to genuinely believe in certain truths or follow ethical standards. Rather, practices that placate the spiritual powers define acceptable human behavior. The focus is upon "arbitrary" techniques for appeasing and manipulating the unseen powers to act in your favor. People fear doing something the wrong way before the spirit world. Leaders in fear-power contexts are often religious or spiritual people believed to be capable of changing the course of history via ritual practices. Though the dynamics of fear and power are commonly associated with tribal shamans or Caribbean voodoo practitioners, they also influence a Brazilian businessman praying to a saint or a Washington politician consulting an astrologer.[9]

Behind the façade of many formal religions stands animism—the functional religion of fear-power cultures. Animism believes spirits which inhabit the physical world (in trees, weather, people, illness, etc.) can be manipulated through magical rituals for personal benefit. These "folk" or "tribal" religions typically observe three dimensions of reality:

1. the seen world (people, houses, physical objects)
2. the unseen of this world (angels, spirits, *mana*, *baraka*, curses, ancestors)
3. the unseen other world (God, heaven, hell)

Since invisible spiritual forces pervade our daily life,

people look to the unseen middle dimension to explain crop failures, illness, accidents, war, or even a child's gender. In 1982, missiologist Paul Hiebert authored "The Flaw of the Excluded Middle" to explain how the Western worldview, influenced by scientific rationalism, excludes the entire middle dimension of spiritual forces in daily life.[10] Modernism dismisses the fear-power worldview as "unscientific superstition," ignoring the real presence of spiritual beings in the world.

Fear-power cultures live in constant fear of invisible powers. They fear a potential misstep may open a vulnerable point for spiritual influence or expose them to harm—such as an accident, a bad dream, or even possession. People in fear-based contexts never know what evil the capricious spirits might inflict. To control the unknowns of life and ward off evil influences, they resort to magical rituals. Secret techniques harness spiritual power to avoid harm and invite blessings. People strive to live in peace with the forces that cohabitate their world. Disharmony with the spiritual could prove disastrous.

Common practices for obtaining power include the use of amulets, curses, charms, fetishes, recitations, incantations, witchcraft, horoscopes, or the evil eye. The moral logic of fear-power cultures says: do something in the seen world to manipulate the unseen world into helping you.

To protect a vulnerable newborn baby from harm, parents may paint an image on her forehead to ward off spirits. To inflict revenge, an offended person may burn a picture of an enemy. To promote fertility, a couple may visit a holy mountain to pray. To contain a contagious disease, the village elders may sacrifice a bull to appease the gods. To ensure prosperity, a family may sacrifice food to ancestors at the family altar. To procure lifelong supernatural influence, a person may purposefully invite dark beings into their life. The voluntary submission to these spirits promises protection, spiritual provision, and perhaps a respected place in the community as a shaman. [11]

The Reason for Culture Types

Why do guilt, shame, and fear cultures exist? The answer is largely socio-economic. The systems through which people acquire resources influence how the group rewards (innocence, honor, power) or punishes (guilt, shame, or fear) its members.

All people must somehow access the basic necessities of life—food, protection, information, health, work, etc. The three primary gatekeepers controlling resources in life are (1) formal institutions, (2) human communities, and (3) unseen spirits. Unless a person can survive entirely alone, he or she must ensure a good relationship with at least one of the gatekeepers. Each system has a unique protocol people must follow to remain in good standing and access resources. For example, let's consider how people obtain directions for driving in each cultural system.

A Western person would probably access a map on their smartphone to get directions. This relies upon legally established institutions and organizations. In this case, the government (U.S. military for GPS info) and corporations (Apple or Google) provide access to directions. To maintain access to the services institutions offer, a person must follow their legal rules and laws. A person guilty of breaking a rule or law is cut off from institutions. In market economies of the West, companies of employment are the primary institutions that provide materially; to keep your job, you must follow HR's policy manual.

In collectivistic societies, people, not institutions, possess information. When living in Central Asia, getting directions was a community-based treasure hunt. My neighbor would only tell me the general direction of my destination: "It's near the green factory across the river." When I arrived at the green factory, I had to ask another person, then another, until I finally arrived. Relational connections are essential for acquiring resources like information, and an honorable reputation ensures those essential relationships. The community does not help or associate with shameful people. Apart from a group, one can hardly access resources essential for living.

Animistic cultures select directions based on unseen spiritual realities. People desire the best *spiritual* route, which can be ensured by consulting a diviner, reciting a magic power, or avoiding dangerous areas. The goal is not speed, but safety.

Since only the spirits know how humans can safely reach their destination, good relationships with the spiritual realm are essential for living life.

Who controls what I need for life: formal institutions, human communities, or spiritual powers? Guilt, shame, and fear are the moral emotions that socio-economic groups use to organize the distribution of resources between people. The three methods of securing directions illustrate how people must be: *innocent* before institutions by obeying the rules and laws, lest they be reckoned guilty, *honorable* in the community by respecting the group's expectations and playing the appropriate roles, lest they be shamed, or *powerful* in the spiritual realm by observing the proper rituals and techniques, lest they be powerless and vulnerable.

This circle illustration visually depicts how a person (in the center) acquires essential resources (the outer ring), and the three potential social barriers.

How Each Culture Meets Human Needs

The economic system of a society influences whether violators primarily experience guilt, shame, or fear. This reality underpins most questions in The Culture Test©. The solution key below explains how each culture type functions in various life situations to meet essential needs. This chart illustrates the practical ways cultures embody their subsurface values. If you have not done so, visit www.TheCultureTest.com to take the free, 5-minute survey before proceeding.

	GUILT	SHAME	FEAR
To get directions, you:	Use a map or GPS	Ask a person	Pray for guidance
Job skills are acquired by:	Formal education	Apprenticing and observing	Receiving sacred knowledge
The sick are best treated by:	A doctor's prescription	A traditional natural remedy	Ritual prayers and sacrifices
An offended person:	Pursues justice	Gets revenge or withdraws	Places a curse
A birthmark is:	Harmless	An embarrassing blemish	An omen or sign
Personal introductions include:	First name and occupation	Full name and title	Alternative name to conceal their birth name
Misdeeds affect the offender's:	Internal conscience	Public reputation	Fate
A trash dump is avoided since it:	Is unhygienic and smelly	Defiles people	Is where spirits reside
The key to starting a good business is:	Writing a good business plan	Having the right contacts	Performing a religious ritual
A dead person's possessions are:	Distributed according to a will	Passed on to family	Buried with the person
People over 70 are socially:	Burdensome	Respected	Powerful

The concept of "family" includes:	Parents, spouse and children	All extended relations	Extended relations and deceased ancestors
Parents often admonish children to:	Fulfill their own interests and passions	Observe community expectations	Appease unseen forces
Truth comes from:	Science and facts	Tradition and consensus	Mysticism and pragmatism.
People taking a road trip:	Take the shortest route	Visit family along the way	Avoid "dark" areas
Infertility is dealt with by:	Finding medical treatment	Getting a new spouse	Visiting a holy person or shrine
Inappropriate behavior causes:	Punishment	Ostracism	Weakness
Weddings usually start:	Near the scheduled time	When key people arrive	At a propitious time or lucky day
Leaders maintain connections w/:	Their followers	Influential people	Spiritual powers
Food is acquired from:	A supermarket	A family farm or local market	Wild nature
People should act according to:	Right and wrong	Roles and expectations	Techniques and tactics
People with money:	Save and invest it	Foster relationships by helping others	Protect it from unfortunate harm
Where a guest sits at a meal:	Is randomly chosen	Indicates their status and age	May affect what happens later
Holy writings provide:	Guidance and instruction	Heritage and identity	Protection and blessing
People get protection from:	Police	Friends	Magical practices
People long for:	Equality and fairness	Status and face	*Security and peace
After misdeeds, people feel:	Remorseful	Inferior	Anxious

Parallel Global Realities

The tripartite classification of guilt, shame, and fear helps us better understand the world as a whole. The three culture types correspond to other global realities. The following chart presents various aspects of the modern world in light of guilt, shame, and fear-based cultures.

Culture Type	Guilt-Innocence	Shame-Honor	Fear-Power
Social Structure	Individualistic	Collectivistic	Animistic
Location	West (North America, Europe)	East (Middle East, Africa, Asia)	South (tribal, Caribbean)
LMR Model (R. Lewis)	Linear-active	Re-active	Multi-active
Religious Status	Post Christian	Minimally Christian	Emerging Christian
Mission Status **% Xian in 1910** **% Xian in 2010**	Were Reached 95% 81%	Unreached 2.7% 8.5%	Now Reached 16% 62%
Population (2010)	1.08 billion	4.37 billion	1.42 billion
Christian Theology	Augustinian, Protestant	Undeveloped	Pentecostal, Charismatic

Some generalizations are certainly oversimplified.[12] For example, honor and shame dynamics significantly shape cultures in southern Europe and tribal people groups. Using the broadest paintbrush creates a definitive outline, but lacks nuance. However, organizing the planet's 7.2 billion people into three categories sheds light on some political and religious features of the modern world.

The correlation between Christian population and theology is missiologically noteworthy. Christianity in the global South mushroomed in the twentieth century, along with Charismatic theology and missiology. Was the Charismatic expression of Christianity the *cause* of church growth in Latin America and Africa? Or is charismaticism the *result* of an established church contextualizing the gospel for its fear-power contexts?

Perhaps the reason for the Church's limited presence in the East is the absence of a theology contextualized for their honor and shame cultures. Most unreached people groups are predominantly honor-shame in cultural orientation. For this reason, a theology for honor-shame cultures may be missiologically strategic for fulfilling the Great Commission of making disciples in all nations.

3
THEOLOGY

The guilt-shame-fear trichotomy additionally serves as a framework for interpreting Scripture and contextualizing theology. This section analyzes the biblical narrative and theological categories from each perspective. Examining the gospel from multiple vantage points can help Christians acquire a fuller understanding of the gospel. Yet we must remember that the Bible is one narrative in which forgiveness, honor, and power are woven together.

The Guilt-Innocence Narrative of Salvation

exchange

God is perfectly holy and just. In all His ways, He acts with perfect righteousness. Sin never enters His presence. This God created the entire world out of nothing.

God created Adam and Eve and placed them in the Garden of Eden. He gave them freedom to eat from any tree, but clearly instructed them to not eat from one tree—the tree of the knowledge of good and evil. But when Adam and Eve disobeyed God's commands, they faced the consequences—physical and spiritual death. They were disciplined for their transgressions. Because of their actions, people are born into a state of sin, naturally opposed to God and his law. Sin separates all people from the holy God. Adam and Eve were banished from the Garden of Eden.   ↑ separate

God gave Israel the Law, which had two main functions. First, the Law revealed to people their moral inadequacy and need for salvation. Israelites were unable to fulfill all of God's commands by their own strength. Human efforts can never reach the divine standard of holiness. Israel's history is one of repeated disobedience and subsequent punishment.

But the Law also included provisions for forgiveness of sins. God provided a means for people to make an atoning sacrifice for their transgressions. Israel's sacrificial system allowed for forgiveness through the ritual sacrifice of spotless animals. The Passover during Israel's exodus from Egypt foreshadowed how shedding blood saves people from God's wrath.

Jesus Christ, God's own Son, became the perfect sacrifice to take away the sins of humanity. Jesus lived a perfectly sinless life. Having no sin of His own, He was able to take our sin. Jesus was the perfect Lamb of God. He was pierced for our transgressions and bore the consequence of our iniquities. Jesus' death on the cross forgives our trespasses and cancels the record of debt that stands against us. Then, Jesus rose from the dead and went to heaven.

God is now building His church from those who repent of their sins and believe in Jesus. To become a follower of Jesus, one must recognize and confess the truth of their sin before God, as moved by the conviction of the Holy Spirit. Because Jesus reconciles us to God, our efforts towards moral perfection are in vain. We are saved by faith as a gracious gift from God, not by our own merit. Being forgiven of our sins, we are called to forgive others. *accepting GRACE - is it really ok?*

When Jesus returns to the earth, God will judge all people justly and punish sin. The wicked will be condemned to hell and the righteous will spend eternity with God in heaven.

The Shame-Honor Narrative of Salvation

God has existed for all of eternity in full glory and honor. He is an honorable King, a Father who provides for the entire family. He is pure, faithful, and glorious—the essence and source of all true honor.

To magnify his glory, God created the world and spoke life into being. From the ground, God created Adam and Eve, crowning them with honor and glory. They possessed authority to rule over creation as God's esteemed co-regents. As God's children, they lived under God's name. Adam and Eve enjoyed an honorable identity from God. They walked naked and were not ashamed.

But Adam and Eve were disloyal to God. They forfeited divine honor to pursue a self-earned honor, Their disloyalty to God created shame, so they hid and covered themselves. Moreover, their sin dishonored God. God lost face. Because Adam and Eve brought shame upon everyone, God banished them from His presence to maintain His dignity.

As descendants of Adam, we inherit their original shame. Then our own defiled and disloyal heart increases shame. This shame shapes our identity and behavior. Sin (i.e., abuse, anger, gossip, boasting, racism, violence, war, etc.) is largely the false attempt to cover shame and fabricate honor. We manufacture a false status, often by shaming others or boasting in the superiority of our own group. Having lost our spiritual face, family, name, and status, our life is a perpetual effort to construct create a new identity a counterfeit honor. As the tower of Babel story illustrates, people seek to exalt themselves and to make a name for themselves. Our shame causes disgraceful conduct and dishonors God.

God then initiated a plan to restore human honor. He covenanted to honor Abra(ha)m with a great name, land, blessing, nation, and many children. As a great nation, Abraham's family would become God's instrument to bless—or honor—all nations. When Abraham's descendants suffered in slavery in Egypt, God delivered them from shameful bondage. Israel became the most prized nation, the apple of God's eye and treasure of His heart.

God made a special covenant to honor Israel, if only she would honor God with loyalty and obedience to Torah. The regulations of Torah cleansed Israelites' defilement and allowed them to be restored to the community. Though God intended for the covenant to produce honor, Israel's frequent disloyalty defamed God's name among the nations. When turning to other gods, she marred God's face as an unworthy spouse. Israel's chosenness led to ethnocentrism—group righteousness. They believed Gentiles were inferior and unworthy to be in God's family. Israel, like Adam, was chosen for honor but ended up in shameful exile. Even though Israel's story ends in national shame, promises and instances of divine exaltation (i.e., Ruth, David, Daniel, and Esther) foreshadow a greater intervention to rescue the human family from shame and restore its honor.

Though He was eternally glorious and honored in heaven as God's son, Jesus became a lowly human being in order to save people from shame. His miraculous healings and radical table fellowship restored dignity and honor to marginalized people. Jesus was so full of divine honor that those who touched him became cleansed and accepted. His teaching proclaimed the true, eternal code of honor. By loving and accepting all people regardless of their reputation, Jesus undercut society's false honor-code, and offered divine honor to humanity. Jesus' life fully honored God.

But Jesus' ministry threatened the earthly honor of established leaders. So they responded by shaming Him, publicly and gruesomely. Jesus was arrested, stripped, mocked, whipped, spat upon, nailed, and hung naked upon a cross before all eyes. He faithfully endured the shame and broke its power. The cross restored God's honor and removed our shame. Face was restored.

God then publicly approved of Jesus' shame-bearing death by resurrecting him to glory. Jesus now sits at God's honorable right hand with a name above all others. Whereas Adam and Israel failed, Jesus succeeded in being truly human; his life honored God and the human family.

Those who give allegiance to Jesus will receive a new status. Their shame is covered and their honor restored. People must renounce games of social manipulation, status construction, and face management to instead trust fully in Jesus for new status. Membership into God's family is not based on ethnicity, reputation, or religious purity, but on one's familial allegiance to the crucified Messiah. God exchanges our old status as unclean, worthless, and inferior outcasts for the status of pure, worthy, and honorable children. Those who follow Christ to the cross of shame will also follow him into resurrection glory.

Being welcomed into God's family allows people to welcome and accept other groups. Christians are able to honor others and glorify God since they possess God's eternal honor and empowering Spirit. Upon Jesus' return, unbelievers will be stripped of all worldly honors and banished to everlasting shame; while believers will receive crowns of eternal honor as God's glory fills all creation. [13]

Key Shame-Honor Verses

The man and his wife were both naked, and they felt no shame. (Gen. 2:25)

For all have sinned and fall short of the glory of God. (Rom. 3:23)

Do not fear, for you will not be ashamed; do not be discouraged, for you will not suffer disgrace; for you will forget the shame of your youth, and the disgrace of your widowhood you will remember no more. (Is. 54:4)

My salvation and my honor depend on God. (Ps. 62:7)

He raises the poor from the dust; he lifts the needy from the ash heap, to sit them with princes and has them inherit a throne of honor. (1 Sam. 2:8)

He was despised and rejected by men, a man of sorrows, and familiar with suffering. Like one from whom men hide their faces he was despised and we esteemed him not. (Is. 53:3)

Jesus endured the cross, disregarding its shame, and has taken his seat at the right hand of the throne of God. (Heb. 12:2)

He humbled himself and become obedient to death—even death on a cross! Therefore, God exalted him to the highest place and gave him the name that is above every name. (Phil. 2:8-9)

As the Scripture says, "Anyone who trusts in him will never be put to shame." (Rom. 10:11)

I have given them the glory that you gave me, that they might be one. (John 17:22)

And whoever believes in him will not be put to shame. So the honor is for you who believe. . . . But you are a chosen race, a royal priesthood, a holy nation, a people for his own possession. . . . Once you were not a people, but now you are God's people. (1 Peter 2:6-10, ESV)

Narratives of Honor: Adam (Gen. 2), Ruth and Naomi (Ruth), Israel (Ez. 16), Hannah (1 Sam. 2), David (2 Sam. 7), Job, Mephibosheth (2 Sam. 9), Esther, the outcasts (Luke 14), the prodigal son (Luke 15), and Jesus (Phil 2:5-11).

The Fear-Power Narrative of Salvation

In the beginning, the creator God made the world by His powerful word. God is sovereign over all creation, the heavens and the earth. In love, He rules with absolute authority and power, and creation praises His mighty strength.

Having made the world as His kingdom, God appointed Adam to reign over the creation. Adam was God's co-regent, the prince of creation. He was given dominion to rule God's creation, symbolized by his right to name the animals. As Sovereign King, God appointed humanity to rule His world.

At some point, a host of spiritual angels rebelled against God's sovereign rule. Satan, the adversary, led the mutiny. The devil schemed to expand his illegitimate power over the earth by bringing humanity under his rule. The crafty serpent wooed Adam and Eve out from God's kingdom into his domain. The rebel forces subjugated humans. Adam's family lost its position of power and authority in the world.

Satan is now the *de facto* ruler. He became the new prince; we were born into his kingdom. People's eyes are blinded and hearts are captured by Satan. Sin, spiritual attack, and idolatry enslave human souls to dark forces.

To reclaim ultimate sovereignty over His kingdom, God selected Israel to be His special instrument in the spiritual battle. Through a covenantal relationship with Israel, God would expand His dominion to all nations. When Israel was oppressed in Egypt, God confronted the Egyptian gods to liberate them from the bondage of Pharaoh. The exodus demonstrated God's power to all people.

God is a mighty warrior, whose heavenly power over evil translates into earthly conquest. When Israel relied upon God, He granted victory regardless of their military disadvantage. But too often they sought power in the wrong places. Israel succumbed to the temptation of false gods in idolatry and occult practices. Instead of depending on the Lord of Hosts, they allied with the gods of Canaan and rulers of larger nations to ensure protection and blessings. Prophets proclaimed and demonstrated God's superiority over the Canaanite gods, but Israel remained powerless to escape Satan's influence.

God's liberating power incarnated in the person of Jesus. He inaugurated God's long-awaited kingdom. Fully empowered by God's spirit, Jesus resisted Satan's offer of co-rulership and remained committed to God's mission of dismantling Satan's kingdom. On an unprecedented scale, Jesus delivered people held captive by Satan. By healing the sick, raising the dead, and casting out demons, Jesus disarmed Beelzebub to plunder his kingdom and set the captives free. Because God was with him, Jesus saved all who were under the power of the devil.

The powers thought killing God's Son would solidify their authority in the world. Their plan backfired. The death of Jesus Christ was the deathblow to evil forces. The cross disarmed the powers and authorities and publicly triumphed over them. Then in the ultimate display of divine power, God resurrected Jesus. Jesus rose from the dead to a position of power and dominion far above all rule and authority.

People must now turn from dark powers and submit to Jesus as Lord. Believers in Jesus are transferred from the kingdom of darkness to the kingdom of light. God raises us up with Christ and seats us with him in the heavenly realms, so that we too have a power and dominion far above all other authorities. God's grace restores our authoritative position in the world. <u>We are co-heirs with Christ.</u>

With constant access to God's Spirit, we now stand firm against Satan. Though Satan continues as a lion on the prowl, Jesus shields us from his evil influence as we affirm our identity and authority in God's anointed Son. God blesses Christians with every spiritual blessing in the heavenly realm, rendering black magic and occult practices spiritually futile. As Christians walk by God's Spirit in faith and love, we conquer the enemy and strip off enslaving sin. The battle concludes when God binds Satan's forces and then rules the world from His throne for all eternity with his people.[14]

Key Fear-Power Verses

"O Sovereign Lord, you have begun to show your servant your greatness and your strong hand. For what god is there in heaven or on earth who can do the deeds and mighty works you do?" (Deut. 3:24)

The god of this age has blinded the minds of unbelievers, so that they cannot see the light of the gospel of the glory of Christ, who is the image of God. (2 Cor. 4:4)

He who does what is sinful is of the devil, because the devil has been sinning from the beginning. The reason the Son of God appeared was to destroy the devil's work. (1 John 3:8)

But if I drive out demons by the Spirit of God, then the Kingdom of God has come upon you. (Matt. 12:28)

And having disarmed the powers and authorities, he made a public spectacle of them, triumphing over them by the cross. (Col. 2:15)

Since the children have flesh and blood, he too shared in their humanity so that by his death he might destroy him who holds the power of death—that is, the devil—and free those who all their lives were held in slavery by their fear of death. (Heb. 2:14-15)

※ For he has rescued us from the dominion of darkness and brought us into the kingdom of the Son he loves. (Col. 1:13)

That power is like the working of his mighty strength, which he exerted in Christ when he raised him from the dead and seated him at this right hand in the heavenly realms, far above all rule and authority, power and dominion. (Eph. 1:19-21, cf. 6:10-18)

✗ For our struggle is not against flesh and blood, but against the rulers, against the authorities, against the powers of this dark world and against the spiritual forces of evil in the heavenly realms. (Eph. 6:12) Be ALERT

The God of Peace will soon crush Satan under your feet. The grace of the Lord Jesus be with you. (Rom. 16:20)

Narratives of Power: Exodus (Ex. 15), Elijah (1 Kg. 18), Jesus' Temptation (Luke 4), Gerasenian (Mark 5), Ephesus (Acts 19), Warrior (Rev. 19).

The Garden of Eden and Sin

The presence of guilt, shame, and fear in global cultures should hardly surprise us. They were all consequences of the first sin in Genesis 3. To understand the biblical narrative of God's 3D salvation, we must properly recognize the multiple dimensions of sin in humankind.

Immediately after the fall, Adam and Eve's eyes were opened. They knew good and evil, right and wrong. Their newfound knowledge evoked a sense of guilt for transgressing God's command. God had instructed them not to eat the fruit from the tree in the middle of the garden, but they broke the only rule in the Garden of Eden. Therefore they lost their innocence and sensed guilt. Right and wrong were internalized in their consciences, and they felt guilty. The transgression of Adam and Eve has impacted humanity throughout history; sinful people alienated from God are incapable of following God's commandments. Though we are all guilty of sinning, God provides a means of forgiveness for His people.

Adam and Eve's disobedience also introduced shame to the world. After disobeying their creator, Adam and Eve covered themselves with fig leaves. They did not want to be seen. They felt unworthy and embarrassed. Before they sinned, Adam and Eve "were both naked, and they felt no shame" (2:25), but now they were naked and ashamed. When God walked about the garden, they hid for the first time. They sensed something wrong with themselves, not just their actions. The shame Adam and Eve felt was not just a private emotion, but also an objective reality. They lost face and status before the rest of creation as they were now associated with pain, weakness, and dirtiness. At death, humans return back to lowly dust. As disloyal children who dishonored God, they lose honor themselves. Ultimately, Adam and Eve were banished from God's community. The human family lost its face. Subsequent children inherit that shame. We sense the dreadful shame of being unacceptable before God. But in His mercy, God provided animal skins for Adam and Eve's nakedness, covering their shame. Throughout the Bible God replaces rejection and disgrace with a renewed honor.

Adam and Eve also felt fear after the fall. When Adam heard God in the garden, he was afraid. Unable to resist the seductive power of Satan, they realized they were truly weak and vulnerable. They did not withstand temptation. Satan now wielded a unique influence in their life. Once ruling as princes over all of God's creation, Adam and Eve must now work the creation like subjugated servants. They become slaves who live in constant fear of their new master. We are vulnerable and defenseless until the Warrior comes to our rescue.

Adam and Eve's original sin introduced guilt, shame, and fear to the world. But God restores innocence, honor, and power to those who trust Him through the atoning life and death of Jesus Christ. "A more biblical understanding of human identity outside of Christ that is framed by guilt, fear, *and* shame will, in turn stimulate a more profound and comprehensive appreciation for the work of Christ on the cross."[15]

The Atonement and Jesus' Death

The atonement explains how the cross makes salvation possible. What happened in the heavenly realm when Jesus died? Historically, Christians have explained the salvific meaning of Jesus' death with various atonement theories. We will describe three theories to see how previous Christians have attempted to contextualize the Bible's teaching and imagery on the atonement for people seeking power, honor, and innocence. [16]

Ransom Theory (Fear)

Human beings are enslaved to an unfit owner and so must be delivered from his bondage. According to early church fathers, God could not simply steal us back, for that would be resorting to the enemy's treacherous ways. A transaction must take place for Satan to release his authority over humans. The price was Jesus, who gave his life as a ransom for humanity (Mark 10:45). Satan took the bait, perceiving victory and ownership over God's Son to be of ultimate worth for his cause. But Satan was unable to exercise authority over Christ as planned. Jesus was not liable to death, so He eluded Satan's control.

Though church fathers expressed the details of the transaction in various ways, their common interpretation of the cross was the triumph of God over evil forces and the liberation of the human race. Contemporary theologians speak of the atonement as "Christus Victor" to emphasize Christ's victory over evil forces. Because of Jesus' death, God has delivered us from fear and granted us spiritual power. The ransom theory was the main atonement theory the first one thousand years of the Church.

Satisfaction (Shame)

All people must honor God by loving and obeying him. We are obligated to pay a debt of honor. Anselm of Canterbury (b. 1033) reasoned that people who fail to rightfully honor God take the honor that is His alone. Because sinners have dishonored God, He must be compensated for loss of face. Humans are incapable of satisfying their honor debt, since honoring God is what is rightly due. Jesus was a substitutionary representative of humanity who fully loved, obeyed, and honored the Father. He satisfied God's impugned honor and eliminates any need to exact punishment. Jesus' death, in essence, saves God's face.[17] The cross further establishes God's honorable character by confirming his Abrahamic promises of global salvation, lest He be regarded as unfaithful or incapable (Rom. 15:8). Anselm's book *Cur Deus Homo*, the primary articulation of the satisfaction theory, reflects the eleventh-century feudal values of personal honor and reparation of dishonor. In this regard, the satisfaction theory was, and is, highly contextualized for shame-honor settings.

Restoring God's glory is the ultimate purpose of the cross, though a secondary consequence of the satisfaction theory is the restoration of human honor. The cross bears our shame (Isa. 53:3) and repairs our face before God. Interestingly, theology developed in eastern Christendom has articulated how Jesus restores glory to humans; Athanasius of Alexandria (b. 296) said, "God became man so man might become God." Eastern Orthodoxy's doctrine of deification (*theosis*) involves divinizing grace that restores the glorious divine image to mankind (cf. John 17:22; 2 Pet 1:4). Jesus' death restores honor to God *and* to people.

Penal Substitution Theory (Guilt)

God is perfectly holy and just, so He must punish transgressions of the law. While God loves us, justice demands a payment for wrongs. According to the penal substitution model, to arbitrarily forgive sin without punishment would make God unjust. Because God is righteous, God always does what is right and gives humans what they deserve. Our sin merits eternal punishment. But Jesus steps into our place as a sacrifice for the wrath due to us. As a propitiation for sins, the cross appeases God's anger against us and pays the debt of our transgressions. Jesus' death pacifies God's wrath against guilty sinners by satisfying the legal requirements of justice. He is the punishment ("penal") in our place ("substitution"). This is how God can acquit the guilty and declare them righteous without compromising his justice.

The penal substitution theory emerged from Reformed legal scholars in the mid-1600s. Since 1800 it has become the dominant atonement theory in Western Christianity, perhaps since it uses the language and values of Western law (esp. retributive justice) to explain how guilty individuals can be legally exonerated in heaven.

Contemporary theology must always prioritize the Bible's imagery and emphases when explaining how Jesus' death on the cross saves people from guilt, shame, and fear. Yet, the various atonement theories from church history can aid our theology.

Systemized Theological Categories

Category	GUILT	SHAME	FEAR
Key Metaphor	Courtroom (legal)	Community (relational)	Combat (military)
Existential Question	How can my sins be forgiven to be assured of heaven?	How can I be a part of the community to be respected?	How can I access the power to control life?
Historical Theology	Augustinian, Reformed	Undeveloped	Pentecostal, Charismatic

GOD			
God	Lawgiver and Judge (sinless, perfect, just)	Father and Patron (faithful, glorious superior)	Ruler and Deliverer (sovereign, transcendent)
God's Holiness	He alone perfectly keeps the absolute moral standard	He alone is worth glory, deserving honor.	He alone created and stands above everything
God's Sovereignty	Forgives transgressors and enacts our future salvation	Honors lowly mortals and humbles the falsely proud	Defeats spiritual opposition and rules the world
God's Righteousness	Punitive justice	Covenantal faithfulness	Cosmic power
SIN			
Sin	Transgression and Lawbreaking	Dishonor and Disloyalty	Insubordination and Idolatry
Sinfulness	Total depravity	Complete unacceptability	Utter vulnerability
Violation	God's laws and justice	God's face and glory	God's power and authority
Sinners	Condemned	Rejected	Cursed
Consequences of Sin	Judgment and punishment	Disgrace and impurity	Domination and bondage
Emotions of Sin	Regret	Unworthiness	Anxiety
The Fall (Gen. 3)	Shifted blame	Covered nakedness	Hid in fear
Cultural Solutions	Justify, confess, restitution	Cover, flee, hide	Animism, black magic
False Hope	Morality, works, merit	Identity, connections, name	Rituals, secrets, charms
OT laws reveal	Our moral failure	Our defilement	Our idolatry

JESUS			
Christ	Substitute and Sacrifice	Mediator and Brother	Conqueror and Liberator
Incarnation	Jesus becomes fully human to pay our debt	Jesus leaves glory to glorify the Father	Jesus arrives to destroy the devil's works
Jesus' Life	Lived sinlessly	Healed the impure, ate with outsiders and Gentiles	Cast out demons, worked miracles, signs and wonders
Jesus' Death	Bears the punishment for our moral transgressions	Removes our shame and restores God's face/honor	Defeats spirits and powers
The Cross	Appeases God's wrath	Changes God's evaluation	Establishes God's Power
Atonement Theory	Penal Substitution	Satisfaction, Theosis	Ransom, Christus Victor
Jesus' Resurrection	Assurance of future salvation	Divine honor for the shamed	Victory over Satan, death
SALVATION			
Salvation	Innocence and Forgiveness	Honor and Face	Power and Freedom
Repentance	From works-righteousness (stop trying to please God with good deeds)	From boasting (resist using cultural systems to promote your status)	From idolatry (abandon false powers and magical rituals)
Grace overcomes	Wickedness	Worthlessness	Weakness
Forgiveness	Pardons wrongs	Reconciles relationships	Removes strongholds
At God's Right Hand	Acceptance and intimacy	Prestige and status	Power and authority
Reconciliation (with God leads to peace with)	Self (soul, conscience)	People (family, community)	Creation (nature, spirits)
Discipleship	Obedience	Loyalty	Submission
Holy Spirit	Guidance for behavior	Communion with Trinity	Empowerment for battle
Ethics	Love Others	Honor Others	Bless Others
Assurance of salvation	Am I saved and morally acceptable?	Am I part of the right community?	Do I have power to overcome dark forces?
Ephesians	2:1-10	2:11-22	6:10-17

4
MINISTRY

In the Bible, God speaks to the primary heart desires of all cultures—innocence, honor, and power. The gospel is truly a multi-faceted diamond capable of rescuing humanity from all aspects of sin.

Our task as Christians is not merely to marvel at the glorious splendor of the diamond, but to spread the knowledge of God's salvation so all nations know the abundant life of God found in Jesus Christ. In this final section, we examine how to do Christian ministry in each cultural context.

Just as people assume the cultural orientation of their context, Christians often assume forms of Christian ministry from the context in which they learned the gospel. We think the methods used to evangelize and make disciples in one context are universally applicable. If we show people the gospel through the wrong lens, it may be a challenge for them to see it. And even if we acknowledge the need for contextualization, we often resort to our default methods of ministry due to a lack of practical alternatives for approaching Christian ministry in diverse cultures.

The three dimensions of global cultures and biblical salvation impact our approach to missions. How can we communicate the gospel as great news in each type of culture? To develop a 3D missiology, we first present two methods of evangelism (the 3D "plan of salvation" and "story of salvation"). Then, to ensure people engage the gospel through meaningful forms, we outline three contextual approaches of Christian witness—truth encounter, power encounter, and community encounter.

The 3D Plan of Salvation

The *Four Spiritual Laws* booklet has touched millions of lives. The tool's simple, 4-part structure shapes how many Christians structure gospel presentations. The following chart uses its familiar structure to suggest the plan of salvation for each culture type. As every context and person is unique, the following are only suggestive evangelistic explanations.

	GUILT-INNOCENCE	SHAME-HONOR	FEAR-POWER
1. God's intention	**God loves you and offers a wonderful plan for our life.** Jesus came so that we would have eternal life and not perish. Jesus offers us an abundant life.	**God values you and wants to honor you as His child.** God created us with glory and honor, to live with harmony in his family.	**God is sovereign and offers you spiritual authority.** God created us to rule his entire creation (seen and unseen) and experience his spiritual blessings.
2. The human problem	**People are sinful and condemned by God.** Our transgressions create a barrier between us and a holy God. Good works fail to reach God's standard.	**People are shameful and dishonor God.** Our rebellion disgraces the glorious God and produces shame. Our attempts to restore honor fall short of covering the shame of our spiritual orphanage.	**People fearfully live under the authority of Satan.** Our idolatry separates us from divine power. The powers of darkness rule over all people, causing sin, death, and harm.
3. The solution of Jesus	**Jesus Christ is the perfect sacrifice for your sins.** Jesus died on the cross in our place to pay the penalty of sins. Jesus bore the wrath of God's punishment for us.	**Jesus Christ bore all your shame and restores honor.** Jesus' disgraceful death removes our shame and restores honor. By honoring God, Jesus allows you to rejoin God's family.	**Jesus is the warrior who restores our power.** Jesus conquered evil powers and death to bring God's power and blessings. His death disarmed powers and provides us spiritual authority.
4. Our Salvific Response	**You must receive Jesus as your personal Savior.** Receive Christ as personal Savior and turn from human morality to have forgiveness of sins and eternal life.	**You must give allegiance to Jesus to enter God's family.** Receive God's gracious welcome into his family and live under His name. Turn from false cultural face to receive God's honor.	**You must know Jesus to access divine power.** Relationally trust Jesus Christ alone for protection and power. Turn from magical rituals and occultism for authority and blessings.

relationship 1st

The 3D Story of Salvation

Each culture type accepts a particular conceptual metaphor as most plausible. That means the language and values from one area of life (i.e., courtroom, community, or combat) are used as metaphors to organize their worldview and spiritual life. Metaphors use images from this world to explain spiritual realities.

The vocabulary lists below reflect specific conceptual metaphors for Christian salvation. People can better understand salvation in Christ when we use the language of culturally plausible metaphors. As an evangelistic exercise, practice telling the biblical story of salvation (i.e., creation, fall, Israel, Jesus, restoration) using the vocabulary of one conceptual metaphor.[18]

Courtroom Language (Guilt)

Law	Transgression	Judgment
Appeasement	Judge	Right/wrong
Rules	Acquittal	Correction
Condemnation	Innocence	Penalty
Sacrifice	Individual	Punishment
Forgiveness	Personal	Merit
Debt	Payment	Commands
Wrath	Guilt	Sacrifice
Justice	Pardon	Works

Community Language (Shame)

Loyalty	Mediator	Family
Father	Jew/Gentile	Community
Child	Harmony	Public
Alliance	Allegiance	Feast
Respect	Unity	Defilement
Inclusion	Hospitality	Humiliation
Face	Reputation	Worth
Reverence	Identity	Acceptance
Dignity	Alienation	Disgraced
Unclean	Approval	Patron(age)
Worthy	Glory	Dishonor
Boasting	Purity	Envy
Threat	Inheritance	Adoption

Combat Language (Fear)

Deliverance	Healing	Satan
Power(s)	Bondage	Authority
Darkness	Domination	Exodus
Magic	Signs	Wonders
Miracles	Possession	Powerful
Weak	Confrontation	Captive
Peace	Power	Almighty
Throne	Control	Oppression
Warfare	Spirits	Holy Spirit
Exorcism	Prayer	Kingdom
Angels	Blessing/Curse	Protection
Deceiver	Freedom	Stronghold
Conquer	Triumph	Idolatry

Contextualized Forms of Witness

Making disciples among shame-based and fear-based cultures involves more than just repacking evangelistic presentations. The channels through which we proclaim the gospel must also be adapted to the cultural context. Communicating God's Word three-dimensionally involves using the forms through which people are accustomed to receiving innocence, honor, and power.

A 3D gospel affects both the *content* of the gospel and the *means* of Christian witness. The conceptual metaphors used in theology (previous section) become the operative metaphors guiding our missiology. How we understand God's mission (i.e., pardoning the guilty, welcoming the shamed, or delivering the fearful) shapes our strategy for Christian ministry.

What would be an appropriate missiological approach to the three cultural orientations? How do people best encounter the gospel? As truth, as power, or as community? People's cultural orientation impacts how they will appreciate and receive the gospel.

In Acts 26:18, Paul describes his mission to the Gentiles in 3D terms—"to open their eyes and turn them from darkness to light, and from the power of Satan to God (*power*), so that they might receive the forgiveness of sins (*innocence*) and a place among those who are sanctified by faith (*honor*) in *Jesus*." Paul's ministry presented a three-dimensional gospel. These three strands of the gospel never function in isolation, but the driving forces of a particular culture may warrant an emphasis on one approach above others. Three encounters during Paul's ministry in the book of Acts illustrate the three approaches to Christian witness—truth encounter, power encounter, and community encounter.

Truth Encounter

During the Sabbath gathering in Antioch of Pisidia (Acts 13:13–42), the synagogue leaders asked Paul to share a word of exhortation. Paul stood and preached how Israel's story has climaxed in the resurrection of Jesus. At the end of his message, Paul challenged, "Therefore, my friends, I want you to know that through Jesus the forgiveness of sins is proclaimed to you." Paul's audience encountered the truth of the gospel.

Western missiology, developed in a cultural setting emphasizing legality, employs courtroom methods for Christian ministry. In a truth encounter, the Christian functions as a legal advocate who verbally explains and defends the truthfulness of the gospel. Proclaiming the gospel involves logically presenting divine truth. Since truth is viewed propositionally, as either right or wrong, one appeals to rationality and reason. As in Acts 13, people are challenged to know the truth and receive forgiveness.

Evangelistic techniques emphasize the proclamation of spiritual "laws." Approaches like "Evangelism Explosion" and

"Romans Road" present the gospel propositionally, appealing to cognitive reason. Apologetics—a popular subject at Christian universities—utilizes philosophy to present the rational basis of the Christian faith and defend against objections. Bestselling apologetic titles like *The Case For Christ* by Lee Strobel or *Evidence that Demands a Verdict* by Josh McDowell illustrate the judicial approach to Christian ministry in guilt-innocence cultures. They present the gospel as truth.

Imparting truth is also how Western Christianity equips believers. The primary form of discipleship—the sermon—assumes values are best transformed through instructional teaching. Western theology favors systematic theology (an orderly and rational account of the Christian faith) and Paul's epistle to the Romans (the most systemized and propositional book of the Bible). These ministry preferences illustrate how the assumptions and methods of judicial courts influence Christian ministry in guilt-innocence contexts.

The missiological approach of truth encounter has produced amazing fruit for God's kingdom, so it remains a key strategy in missions. The world must continue to hear the truth of the gospel. Yet Christians from guilt-innocence contexts must be aware of how their default cultural orientation influences their missiological methods. Majority World cultures may better encounter God's salvation through power and community.

Power Encounter

When Paul and Barnabas left Antioch on their first journey, they arrived on the island of Cyprus. The proconsul summoned Barnabas and Paul to share the word of God, but a local magician began to oppose their message. Paul immediately recognized the dark spiritual forces behind the magician's words and commissioned the Lord's hand against him. The proconsul saw how the magician's eyes were blinded, then believed their teaching about the Lord. The proconsul on Cyprus encountered the power of the gospel in Acts 13:4-12.

Fear-power cultures may require power proof, not rational reasoning, to believe the Lordship of Christ. People must tangibly see the power of God in daily life. In the power encounter approach, missions is a spiritual battle.

Christians are God's forces battling to overcome Satan's strongholds and expand God's reign. The Church rescues people from the domain of darkness into the kingdom of Jesus. Believers filled with God's Spirit combat the enslaving power of Satan with the liberating power of God. Evangelism is a power encounter in which converts move from the realm of one spiritual authority to another. The original battle is between God and Satan for control and worship, but it is played out here on earth. In this regard, spiritual warfare appropriates the heavenly victory won by Jesus for life on earth.

The primary instruments of spiritual warfare are God's

Word and prayer. The promises of God's Word provide the spiritual resources to withstand the deception and lies of Satan's false kingdom. Prayer, when coupled with genuine faith, replaces magic rituals and sacred objects as channels of supernatural influence. Prayer relationally asks the Sovereign Creator to expand His glorious kingdom by blessing his saints on earth.

Christians can apply the divine power accessed through Scripture and prayer in several ways.

1. Counseling ministries disciple Christians to overcome sinful bonds with knowledge of God's spiritual resources and true identity in Christ. In discerning satanic deception and internal healing, believers experience God's deliverance from spiritual oppression and sin.

2. Signs and wonders are visible miracles manifesting the power of God's Spirit among unbelievers. Jesus' disciples have authority to overcome forces of darkness by praying in Jesus' name.

3. Prophecy refers to direct, spiritual words of instruction or encouragement, demonstrating the knowledge and power of God's Spirit.

4. Public confrontations challenge the power of ancestral gods and prove the superiority of the Creator God, like the encounters between Moses and Pharaoh (Exodus 7-12) or Elijah and the Baal prophets (1 Kings 18).

5. Dreams are often interpreted as revelation from God.

Reports indicate many Muslims turn to Christ after seeing Jesus in a dream. When discussions with Muslims become argumentative, I sometimes redirect the conversation by saying, "I will pray for Jesus to come to you in a dream. When he does, give me a call."

People can experience the good news of God's power through counseling, signs and wonders, prophecy, public confrontations, and dreams. Christian mission in fear-power contexts can present the gospel by manifesting God's power in such contextually appropriate ways.[19]

Community Encounter

Paul and Silas sat in their prison cell, singing and praying to God. Suddenly, an earthquake rattled the prison doors open and unshackled their handcuffs. The jailer on duty awoke to the chaos and drew his sword to kill himself, having failed his duties. Paul shouted just in time "Stop! We are here!" After the situation settled down, the jailer and his household came to believe in the Lord Jesus for salvation, then enjoyed an evening of fellowship together with Paul and Silas. In Acts 16, the Philippian jailer's family believed in Jesus when they encountered the gospel as community.

In shame-honor contexts, Christian mission brings people to encounter true community. A community encounter redefines a person's primary group identity through genuine relationships.

Entrance into a new community transforms one's spiritual status. Conversion means granting loyalty and allegiance to a new group—God and His people. Through a community encounter, unbelievers come to redefine their court of reputation (i.e., who decides which people are honorable) and honor code (i.e., what is truly honorable and shameful) in light of God's honor. A biblical community encounter involves the interface of three groups: the Trinity, the Church, and family.

The Trinity

Christian mission leads people to encounter The Most Honorable and Glorious. Honor is reoriented around the Triune community. Father, Son, and Spirit replace family, ethnicity, and tribe as the community of honor. The Father welcomes home the shamed with a gracious acceptance and honor. The Son now functions as our honorable Brother, saving a seat of honor for us in heaven. The Spirit comes as a down payment of our future inheritance of glory. True face only comes from encountering the Face of God. Relationally knowing God's Face, as revealed in the face of Jesus, is the only definitive source for gaining a new and esteemed status.[20]

The Philippian jailer sought to kill himself to cover his shameful failure on the job. Like a Japanese warrior, he acted to preserve the honor of his people by sacrificing his own life. People in honor-shame cultures must come to acknowledge the falseness of social shame, even though initially it may be very painful. With his sword drawn, the Philippian jailer paused long enough to reconsider how God's honor outweighs all possible social shame.

Eternal glory comes solely through God's Son (John 17:22), because only God's opinion will last forever. When people reject God as the lone source and arbiter of honor, they chose finite honor over infinite glory (John 12:42–43). Christian mission replaces false shame ("I am a worthless nobody.") and false honor ("My group is best!") with true honor from God.

The Church

To save the jailer's life, Paul yelled out, "We are here!" The church, as the earthly body of Christ, is the primary community in which unbelievers encounter the gospel. While ultimate honor comes from God, participation in God's family on earth is where honor is remade, affirmed, and expressed. The Christian community affirms peoples' honor. The church functions as a surrogate family whose gracious welcome frees people to unmask their shame.

The conversation process of shame-honor people generally starts with community (i.e., community □ evangelism), whereas truth encounter begins by evangelizing individuals into the church (evangelism □ community). Group-oriented people must experience the group before accepting an invitation to join it.

New Testament authors commonly equate incorporation into God's community with Christian salvation. "And whoever believes in him will not be put to shame. So the honor is for you who believe. . . . But you are a chosen race, a royal priesthood, a holy nation, a people for his own possession. . . . Once you were not a people, but now you are God's people" (1 Pet. 2:6–10, ESV).

When presenting the gospel in shame-honor cultures, believers' relational bridges with unbelievers must dignify and honor. The way we engage people must align with the message we proclaim by tangibly embodying God's honor. Mediating true honor in both word and deed is essential for reaching people in honor-shame contexts. Shaming people, even unintentionally, contradicts the gospel of God's honor. Here are four ways to relationally mediate God's honor to people and communities.

The Philippian jailer sensed God's honor best through his relationship with Paul and Silas. By not fleeing jail, they sacrificed their own lives and reputation to preserve his honor. Then they graciously accepted the jailer's invitation to eat together. Sharing a meal is one effective way to honor others, since it forms a relational bond. Table fellowship was a central way Jesus honored the marginalized in the Gospels (Luke 15:1). A shared table preaches God's honor as loudly as a sermon in collectivistic societies.

A good development project creates opportunities for people to express the honorable aspects of their personality and culture. The approach of asset-based community development (ABCD) honors people by emphasizing their assets and social capital.[21] Unfortunately, some Christian development efforts perpetuate shame by beginning with people's needs and poverty. Always being on the receiving end of relationships reinforces messages of inferiority and worthlessness.

A fourth way to honor people relationally is to address conflict honorably. Christians living in honor-shame cultures must learn to resolve conflict without offending or exposing others. If you offend someone, helping him or her somehow restore honor may be more appropriate than verbally apologizing. Or to communicate forgiveness to others, consider nonverbal forms of reconciliation, such as a gift or meal. Paying attention to the dynamics of face and reputation during conflict, and not focusing solely on right and wrong, preserves and restores relationships.[22]

Eating together, asset-based community development, mercy ministries, and gracious conflict resolution represent several tangible ways the Church can communicate honor.

The Family

In collectivistic cultures, conversion to Christianity may shame one's biological family and neighboring community. Many unreached peoples do not reject Christianity for theological reasons but because of social and cultural forces that disgrace one's family. For collectivistic people, choosing their religion in isolation from the group implies rejection of the group itself. I recall several Central Asian unbelievers who acknowledged their shame before God and realized Jesus was the only path to eternal honor, but were nevertheless unwilling to risk their community standing or family's reputation to follow Jesus. Because of social shame, a gospel message repackaged in the language of honor and shame will probably not become a magic key for unlocking doors. Christian ministry in honor-shame contexts must also contextualize the evangelistic methods and conversion process.

While faith in Christ is always personal and might include rejecting group obligations, there are New Testament examples of family conversions. Paul's invitation for the jailer's entire family to be saved avoided the scandal of one person disgracing the rest of the family. The idea of "group conversion" does not ignore individual faith and repentance but understands some people prefer to make decisions in a group setting, interdependently and simultaneously. Turning to Christ through a group experience limits unnecessary social dislocation.[23]

The notion of interdependent decisions for Christ impacts our evangelism. For example, if a young person indicates interest in Jesus, it may be prudent to invite the entire family into the conversation. By sharing with the household leader and anticipating a family decision to follow Christ, we will limit the social upheaval of extracting an individual from their community. A missiological approach of community encounter involves helping people encounter Jesus as a community, not just individually.

Nevertheless, some people in shame-honor societies will individually decide to follow Christ. This often produces family arguments, angry threats, and community gossip. Amidst those challenging circumstances, there may be long-term advantages to encouraging new believers to remain in their family as a light and not disdain social customs. Family networks are the most natural channels for transmitting the gospel in shame-honor contexts, so they should be maintained whenever possible. Extracting new converts from their social networks limits their influence as Christians. In Central Asia, we discovered nearly 70% of Christians came to Jesus through a believing relative. A study in Thailand concluded the odds of an unbeliever becoming a Christian are 229 times higher if they have a Christian relative.[24]

People in shame-honor cultures can meaningfully experience the gospel by encountering the divine and ecclesial community from within their social network.

5
CONCLUSION

Sin distorts the human family by causing guilt, shame, and fear. Consequently, the cultures of the world chase after innocence, honor, and power apart from God. But the God of the Bible desires to bless all peoples with the fullness of salvation in Christ. The calling of the Church is to meaningfully introduce the nations to the God who addresses our deepest cultural and spiritual longings.

But the 3D gospel is for Christians, especially those in ministry, just as much as for unreached cultures. Theological tunnel vision that only sees one facet of the diamond shackles our own relationship with God. Western Christians may fully trust in Jesus for the forgiveness of sins, and yet be plagued by shame and fear. Christians often feel ashamed for "not being good enough" and try to mask apparent deficiencies. Feeling inadequate or worthless because of past hurts or recent failures hinders our intimacy with God. Fear also animates Western culture. We may not worry about spiritual forces afflicting us, but we do feel anxious about the future. This fear drives us to find security and protection in "modern" powers (i.e., The Department of Homeland Security, Charles Schwab, 401(k), etc.). Before we proclaim a 3D gospel, we must experience and represent it in our own life.[25]

More significantly, a one-dimensional gospel threatens the veracity and integrity of the Bible. We misread Scripture and construct a sub-biblical view of God. If God does not save us from shame and fear (not just theoretically, but practically), then we severely minimize his glory as God. A 3D gospel allows us to more fully worship our holy, glorious, and sovereign God.

As we grasp all dimensions of the gospel, we can more effectively know God and make him known. In closing, "I pray that the eyes of your heart may be enlightened in order that you may know (*and proclaim*) the hope to which he has called you, the riches of his glorious inheritance in the saints, and his incomparably great power for us who believe" (Ephesians 1:18-19). Amen!

("3D GOSPEL VERSE")

Discussion & Reflection Questions

Culture (ch 2)

1. In your ministry context, where do you see elements of guilt, shame, and fear?

2. What are good and bad elements of each culture type?

3. Give an example of a "cultural miscue," when you (or someone else) misread a situation because of different cultural values.

Theology (ch 3) GR EAT !

1. What biblical passage or theological doctrine do you better understand now?

2. How might you explain the relationship between the three dimensions of salvation (i.e., forgiveness, honor, and power)?

3. What is one verse or story you want to memorize?

Ministry (ch 4)

1. What truths from this book might resonate with people in your ministry context?

2. How could you adapt your ministry so that people encounter the gospel through relationships and spiritual power?

3. Give a short explanation of the gospel in terms of honor-shame (or fear-power), without looking at the book.

More Resources by Jayson Georges

The website **www.HonorShame.com** offers free ministry tools, training videos, journal articles, and more. Subscribe to the weekly blog to get the latest resources.

The series ***Honor-Shame Paraphrase*** helps readers understand the Bible according to its original, non-Western context. Each book unlocks the meaning of Scripture in insightful and accessible ways. Learn more at HonorShame.com/HSP or Amazon.com.

The book ***Ministering in Honor-Shame Cultures*** (InterVarsity Press, 2016. 272 pages) presents a full biblical theology of honor and shame, along with many practical advice and case studies for keys aspects of Christian mission.

Notes

1 Eugene Nida, *Customs and Cultures* (New York: Harper, 1954), 150. This tripartite division of culture was initiated by Nida, then expanded and popularized by Roland Muller, *Honor and Shame: Unlocking the Door* (Philadelphia: Xlibris, 2001).

2 "Groupality," *Wikipedia*, October 1, 2014, http://en.wiktionary.org/wiki/groupality.

3 For further reading on Ephesians, see: Clint Arnold, *Power and Magic: The Concept of Power in Ephesians* (Eugene, OR: Wipf and Stock, 2001); Peter Gosnell, "Honor and Shame Rhetoric as a Unifying Motif in Ephesians," *Bulletin for Biblical Research* 16:1 (2006): 105–128.

4 Muller, *Honor and Shame*, 16.

5 "Uncle Calls Boston Marathon Bombers 'Losers'," *CNN*, April 19, 2013,
http://www.cnn.com/2013/04/19/us/marathon-suspects-uncle/index.html.

6 Alexandra Garcia and Sergio Pecanha, "World Cup Despair in Brazil," *The New York Times*, July 9, 2014.

7 Wesley Yang, "'Tiger Writing,' by Gish Jen," *The New York Times*, April 26, 2013.

8 For further reading, see: "Understanding 8 Traits of Honor-Shame Cultures," *www.HonorShame.com*, April 17, 2014, http://honorshame.com/understanding-8-traits-of-honorshame-cultures/; "The Chase for Face: The Shame of Western Collectivism," Jackson Wu, August 19, 2014, http://www.washingtoninst.org/8618/the-chase-for-face-the-shame-of-western-collectivism/; David deSilva, *Honor, Patronage, Kinship, and Purity* (Downers Grove, IL: InterVarsity Press, 2000).

9 Steven V. Roberts, "White House Confirms Reagans Follow Astrology, Up to a Point," The New York Times, May 4, 1988.

10 Paul Hiebert, "The Flaw of the Excluded Middle," *Missiology* 10:1 (1982): 35-47.

11 For further reading, see: Dean Halverson, "Animism: The Religion of the Tribal World" *IJFM* 15:2 (1998): 59-67; Gailyn Van Rheenen, *Communicating Christ in Animistic Contexts* (Pasadena, CA: William Carey Library, 1996); Paul Hiebert, Daniel Shaw, and Tite Tienou, *Understanding Folk Religion* (Grand Rapids, MI: Baker Academic, 2000).

12 Statistics regarding population and religion were compiled from data in Todd Johnson and Kenneth Ross, eds., *Atlas of Global Christianity* (Edinburgh University Press, 2009). "Christian" for South America includes evangelical and charismatic Christians (whether Roman Catholic or Protestant) so excludes nominal figures. Samuel Huntington, *The Clash of Civilizations and Remaking of World Order* (New York: Simon & Schuster, 1997); Richard Lewis, *When Cultures Collide*, 3rd ed. (Boston, MA: Nicholas Brealey Publishing, 2005).

13 For further reading, see: Jason Borges, "'Dignified': An Exegetical Soteriology of Divine Honour," *Scottish Journal of Theology* 66:1 (2013): 74–87; Jayson Georges, "From Shame to Honor: A Theological Reading of Romans for Honor-Shame Contexts," *Missiology* 38:3 (2010): 295–307; Edward T. Welch, *Shame Interrupted* (Greensboro, NC: New Growth Press, 2012); Werner Mischke, *The Global Gospel* (Scottsdale, AR: Mission ONE, 2015). For concise videos presenting the biblical narrative in honor-shame language, view "How Does God Seek Face?" by Jackson Wu and "Back to God's Village" by HonorShame.com, both available on *YouTube.com*.

14 For further reading, see: Tom Julien, *The Three Princes: Lifting the Veil on the Unseen World* (Winona Lake, IN: BMH, 2011); Tremper Longman III, "The Divine Warrior: The NT Use of an OT Motif," *Westminster Theological Journal* 44 (1982): 290-307.

15 Timothy Tennent, *Theology in the Context of World Christianity: How the Global Church Is Influencing the Way We Think about and Discuss Theology* (Grand Rapids, MI: Zondervan, 2007), 92.

16 For further reading, see: Joel Green and Mark Baker, *Recovering The Scandal of the Cross: Atonement in the NT and Contemporary Contexts*, 2nd ed. (Downers Grove, IL; InterVarsity Press, 2011); J.I. Packer, *The Logic of Penal Substitution*, (Fig, 2012).

17 Jackson Wu, *Saving God's Face: A Chinese Contextualization of Salvation Through Honor and Shame* (Pasadena, CA: William Carey, 2012).

18 The 3 semantic fields were adapted with permission from an unpublished paper of Dr. Tom Steffen. For further reading, Craig Ott, "The Power of Biblical Metaphors for Contextualizing the Gospel," *Missiology* 42:4 (2014): 357-374.

19 For further reading, see: Neil Anderson and Timothy Warner, *Beginner's Guide to Spiritual Warfare* (Ventura, CA: Regal, 2008); Clint Arnold, *3 Crucial Questions about Spiritual Warfare* (Grand Rapids, MI: Baker Academic, 1997); Doug Hayward, "The Evangelization of Animists: Power, Truth or Love Encounter?" *IJFM* 14:4 (1997): 155-159.

20 Christopher L. Flanders, *About Face: Rethinking Face for 21st Century Mission* (Eugene, OR: Wipf & Stock Pub, 2011).

21 Robert D. Lupton, *Toxic Charity: How Churches and Charities Hurt Those They Help, And How to Reverse It* (New York, NY: HarperOne, 2012); Steve Corbett and Brian Fikkert, *When Helping Hurts: How to Alleviate Poverty Without Hurting the Poor . . . and Yourself* (Chicago, IL: Moody Publishers, 2012).

22 Duane Elmer's excellent book *Cross-Cultural Conflict* (Downers Grove, IL: InterVarsity Press, 1993) helps Christians wisely resolve conflict in honor-shame contexts.

23 Tennent, *Theology in the Context of World Christianity*, 97-99.

24 Marten Visser, *Conversion Growth of Protestant Churches in Thailand* (Zoetermeer, 2008), 123.

25 For further learning, see: "3D Gospel," *Hope Church* (Oakdale, MN), March 16, 2014,
http://www.hopechurchoakdale.com/2014/03/3d-gospel-march-16-2014/; Brene Brown,
"Listening to Shame", *TED*, March 2012,
http://www.ted.com/talks/brene_brown_listening_to_shame.

Made in the USA
Lexington, KY
18 October 2018